Early Days on the Great Lakes

*The Art of
William Armstrong*

Luggar rigged fishing boat.

Schooner yacht Oriole II.

Early Days on the Great Lakes
The Art of William Armstrong

Henry C. Campbell

McClelland and Stewart Limited
Toronto/Montreal

0-7710-1887-8

The Canadian Publishers
McClelland and Stewart Limited
25 Hollinger Road, Toronto 374

Printed and bound in Hong Kong

Contents

Acknowledgements

The information in this book has been gathered almost entirely by relying on the evidence of William Armstrong's paintings. This, understandably, is not the most accurate method, but for lack of other documentary sources, was the one which had to be adopted. The various possibilities of conflicts and errors that this can result in are freely admitted.

I have been fortunate in receiving the full help and assistance of many people. I am indebted to friends of the Armstrong family as well as to descendants of his children who have generously supplied whatever information they could, and particularly to Mrs. Freda Lawson.

Because several versions of a painting are often available, the choice of the one to be reproduced has, in many cases, been based on its suitability for reproduction. The drawings from *The Canadian Illustrated News* are all from sketches by William Armstrong. In some instances, only a portion of a picture has been used.

Mr. J. Russell Harper, Mr. Michael Bell, Mrs. Helene Ignatieff, and Mrs. Mary Alodi have generously provided me with information at their disposal. I am grateful to the Sigmund Samuel Gallery, the Glenbow Alberta Institute, and the Metropolitan Toronto Library Board and other co-operating institutions for the use of materials in their collections.

Mrs. P. C. Band, the Royal Canadian Yacht Club, Toronto, the Marine Museum of the Toronto Historical Board, and the Winnipeg Art Gallery also have been most generous in providing materials. I am especially grateful to Dr. Frank N. Walker for his interest and suggestions concerning the work of Armstrong for the Grand Trunk Railways, and to Mr. Alan Suddon for unearthing the story of Armstrong's microfilming exploits. I also am grateful to Miss Raye Howard and staff members of the Toronto Public Library Board, who assisted in many ways in seeing this work to its completion.

The east side of Thunder Cape, looking north.

William Armstrong – Artist and Engineer

In a young land obsessed with growth and newness, it was perhaps inevitable that Canada should have lost sight not only of William Armstrong but of the age which as an engineer he helped shape and as an artist he set out to preserve. And yet it was in Victorian Canada that the foundations of modern Canada were built, and William Armstrong typified the industrious spirit of that time.

During the mid- and late-1800's, Canada's manufacturing and commercial empires were born; its natural resources tapped; its cities grew and the railways fingered out from the settled east to embrace the prairies and the west. It was a time of the marriage of vaunting imagination and the new industrial technology which enabled Victorian Canada to make the leap from a colonial enclave hugging the Atlantic and lower Great Lakes to ocean-linking nationhood.

William Armstrong's contribution to this was unique. Other men were more notable railroaders; still others were better artists. But Armstrong combined the talents of an inventor, a builder, a draughtsman, a skilled engineer and designer shaped by the Industrial Revolution, and a man of imagination who looked at Victorian Canada with the eyes of an artist. He helped build the railroads which bound an immensity of land into a whole, and he made his own contribution to the development of Canadian art and graphic illustration.

Any Irishman's future was bleak when William Armstrong was born on July 28, 1822, in Dublin. For the younger son in a middle-class family (William was the seventh son of a distinguished army officer), the only way to find an opportunity to prosper was to go in search of it, usually to England or the colonies. At sixteen William, already displaying some artistic aptitude, was sent to England as an apprentice to Thomas Jackson Woodhouse, chief engineer of the Midland Counties Railway. After spending three years with Woodhouse, young William had become a recognized draughtsman and designer, seasoned in planning bridges and sections for the British railways. It was this experience in seeing how the railway brought the country nearer to the town, and the town to the country, that provided Armstrong with his life-long interest in portraying the impact of transportation on the people and the land.

His apprenticeship ended, he moved to London as draughtsman and office manager for an engineering firm. But his love of Ireland lingered, and in 1842, at the age of twenty, he returned to Dublin to marry Lucy Kirby Daniell of County Wicklow.

The Industrial Revolution created the grimy, unlovely industrial towns and cities stretching across England, and the Armstrongs saw some of the worst of them. As a railway draughtsman, he spent time in Derby, Rugby, Nottingham and Leicester; as a husband and father, he lived in London, Accrington and Liverpool. He and Lucy moved to Accrington soon after their marriage, and it was here that their first child, Berdée, was born in 1846. Two years later they moved to Liverpool, where William worked as an engineer on the Birkenhead docks. And it was from Liverpool that the Armstrongs decided to escape. First they tried to settle back in Dublin, but in 1851, frustrated by the lack of opportunity, he and Lucy decided to emigrate to Canada.

Since he came well recommended by English railway builders, William Armstrong soon met the Canadian leaders in that profession. He began his engineering career with the Northern Railway Company in Toronto, working under the direction of Frederick W. Cumberland. In the 1850's, Colonel (later Sir) Casimir Gzowski's firm was building the Toronto-Sarnia portion of the Grand Trunk Railway, at that time the biggest railroading enterprise in Canada. He became a friend of Sandford Fleming and later travelled with Fleming in connection with the building of the Canadian transcontinental railway.

Armstrong thrived in Canada. He helped organize the Royal Canadian Yacht Club of Toronto, joined the Anglican Church, became a member of the Loyal Orange Lodge, found a site for a home on Toronto Island, painted the city as he saw it from there, and entered one of these paintings in a contest of the Mechanics Institute. He didn't win, but five years later the Toronto City Council paid him £130 for a painting which was hand-lithographed and coloured and proudly distributed to other municipalities.

In 1855 his drawings were exhibited at the Paris Universal Exposition; he won first prize for the best collection of photographed landscapes at the Provincial Exhibition in Toronto in 1862; and in 1865 he sent a collection of water colours of twenty-seven Indian chiefs and views of Lake Superior to the Canadian display at the Dublin Exhibition. All his life he painted mainly in water colours, turning out many hundreds of views.

For his sketching and painting expeditions, and on his civil engineering travels, Armstrong explored the little-known reaches of the Great Lakes on the steamers of the Lake Superior Royal Mail which sailed from Collingwood on Georgian Bay and from Sault Ste. Marie on Lake Superior. It was a geographic quirk that, to go west, the railways first had to go north to skirt Superior if they were to be built on Canadian territory. And always Armstrong took photographs and drew and painted. Years later he was to claim that his drawings of northwest Canada induced some mining companies to open up the area.

He even got involved in the shadowy world of espionage during the American Civil War, and introduced micro-photography to the business of spying. A group of Confederate army officers then in Toronto wanted to send a vital message to Jefferson Davis, president of the secessionist Confederacy. As Armstrong explained it years later: "I suggested the reducing of the message by photography onto mica, which plan was adopted. I printed in large letters on a flat paper the message and reduced it to the size of five buttons. The negatives were then placed under the usual coverings of buttons by Mr. Walker, tailor of King Street. The messenger wore the coat and got through."

In 1870 William Armstrong embarked on an adventure that was to become one of the epics of Canadian history. He joined the military expedition under Colonel Garnet Wolseley that was sent to subdue Louis Riel and his followers, then in open rebellion at Fort Garry. His help in engineering was needed to enable the troops to negotiate the rivers and lakes of northwestern Ontario. He was given the rank of captain in the 63rd Regiment and was made chief engineer.

It was to change his life. *The Canadian Illustrated News* published his drawings and sketches of the Red River Expedition and they earned him widespread recognition as an artist. By the early 1880's, he had won sufficient acknowledgement to be made an associate of the Royal Canadian Academy. But he remained something of a maverick: he quit the Academy soon after becoming an associate, claiming that the selection of pictures to be hung was unfair.

William Armstrong was not, of course, the only artist whose work recorded the westward move of Victorian Canada. But while most of his contemporaries — Daniel Fowler, T. Mower Martin, O. R. Jacobi and, among others, John Arthur Fraser — turned to other subjects, William Armstrong confined himself almost exclusively to landscapes and to recording the monuments of the industrial age and their effects on both Indians and the scattered communities of settlers. He chose to paint ships, trains, bridges, railroad stations, waterworks and factories; the Indians as the pioneering railroads found them; the misty panoramas of his new and immense homeland. Almost always there were human figures in his work, but rarely as the focal point. Indeed, the few portraits he did paint are not as satisfactory as his landscapes.

The influence of his training as an engineer is always evident. There is a precision, almost a geometric severity, to his work. His work is not photographic, but neither is it in the romantic tradition of those artists whose paintings glamourized and softened the raw and rugged land that was Canada. William Armstrong was content to strive for the true characteristics of the topographical artist, to go down in history as an adventurous traveller who made an accurate record of his discoveries.

William Armstrong died in Toronto on June 8, 1914. Surviving him were his wife Lucy, his four daughters Berdée, Maude, Rose, Nenon and his sons Victor, Claude and Arthur Harrie. It was as though the end of their life together was also the end of life itself for Lucy: she died barely a year later and was buried alongside him in the Anglican Cemetery of St. John's Norway in Toronto.

William Armstrong, about 1860.

Lucy Daniell Armstrong, about 1860.

The Armstrongs had a firm stake in the life of Canada. By 1870 they had had eleven children, and in that year, to have more time for his family, William Armstrong began teaching drawing at the Toronto Model School, and later at the Collegiate Institute and elsewhere. He did not entirely abandon civil engineering, but for the next twenty-six years, he was more teacher and artist than engineer and businessman.

The "Priory," 15 Esther Street, Toronto, 1896.

The Armstrongs' first home in Toronto was a small cottage on John Street, just north of Queen. Contemporaries later said the circular saw he had shipped across from Ireland for use in a sawmill lay rusting in front of the cottage for some time. Two years later, William and Lucy moved to their new home, the Priory, on what is now Augusta Avenue. They loved it so well that they never moved. They or their children lived there for more than eighty years, and it was a landmark in Victorian Toronto.

Armstrong set up his first studio on Church Street five years after he arrived in Toronto, but in 1859 he moved to 42 King Street East, near Yonge. It was here that the firm of Armstrong, Beere and Hime, engineers and photographers, received many assignments to sketch and photograph industrial and engineering achievements of the day.

View looking north from Armstrong's studio, King Street East, Toronto, about 1861.

Around him William Armstrong watched the changes that industrial growth was bringing to Canada. The coal yard on the Toronto waterfront became a symbol of the ascendant place of commerce over nature. Armstrong's life was bound up with the developments that mining and the railways brought to Canada.

Ontario Coal Company wharf, Toronto, 1891.

William Armstrong (right) was 92 when he died.

The Grand Trunk Railway bridge over the Credit River at Georgetown, Canada West.

Building the Railways

William Armstrong arrived in Toronto several months before railway construction northward and westward began with an advertisement in city newspapers by the Ontario, Simcoe and Huron Railway Company. Tenders were invited for clearing, grading, bridging and other work on a line to Barrie on the western edge of Lake Simcoe.

October 15, 1851, was the day on which the first sod was turned for the new rail line–and it was declared a public holiday by the City of Toronto. Almost twenty thousand people crowded around the city hall, then on Front Street, as Lady Elgin, the wife of the Governor General performed the ceremony.

Public interest was exhibited wherever the railroad went. In May, 1853, the lines had reached Machell's Corners, near present-day Aurora, and on May 16, the first train left Toronto. All the way to Machell's Corners crowds turned out to cheer, and there was a great celebration when, two hours later, the train gave its final puff of steam and stopped at its destination.

The railways brought development everywhere. The Ontario, Simcoe and Huron, or the Northern Railway, as it became, pushed north from Barrie to Lake Huron, choosing as its terminus a place called the Hen and Chicken's Harbour. This name came from a scattering of offshore islands. By Christmas, 1853, there were only four families in Hen and Chicken's Harbour, plus fisherman William Watts and the few men he employed. Through 1854 boarding houses and taverns for railway workers sprang up in the bush. On January 1, 1855, the first train ran from Barrie to the new terminus, and Hen and Chicken's Harbour, renamed Collingwood, became a bustling shipping and shipbuilding town. Steamships ran from Collingwood to all of the ports on the lakes.

Another line on which William Armstrong worked was the Grand Trunk Railway, which linked Montreal and Toronto in 1856. Armstrong supervised the drawing of building plans both for the section of line which by 1859 ran from Toronto to the U.S. border at Sarnia, and for the extension to Detroit, opened in 1861.

Through the 1860's and 1870's, rail lines laced the countryside around Toronto. There was the Toronto, Grey and Bruce Railway, the Toronto and Nipissing Railway, the Great Western and others. Many companies competed in the bid to circle the Great Lakes and head west to the Pacific, and William Armstrong's draughting talent was in constant demand in supervising the preparation of the drawings used in construction work. He worked on the plans for bridges, viaducts, stations; he patented his own design of a wood-loading device for use by the Grand Trunk Railway's locomotives in 1860. The events and incidents in the railway expansion were widely published by the popular illustrated periodicals of the day, and Armstrong's drawings appeared regularly in *The Canadian Illustrated News* from 1870 to 1874.

In the space of twenty years, the railways welded the scattered communities of what was then called Canada West into a homogenous whole. Men no longer measured distance in miles, but in the cost of a train ticket.

The importance of railways to Canada as a nation can be
measured by the location and design of the stations
in every city and town in the country. Yet the early stations
were anything but great architectural inspirations.
Even in Toronto, the depot below Front Street, opened
in 1858 to serve the Grand Trunk, the Great Western and the
Northern Railway lines, was uncomfortably modest.

Toronto Grand Trunk Railway Station, 1857.

Railways came to Canada West only after 1850 and so people were well aware of their significance long before the twin rails snaked their way through their communities. The impact of Stephenson's locomotive on both the social and economic life of Britain and Europe was widely noted in the newspapers and periodicals of the mid-1800's, and even closer to home, the U.S. railways had wrought major changes south of the border. For the pioneer settlers of Canada West–that part of the nation now better described as Ontario–they meant more than easier access to the markets where their produce and products could be sold; they also meant an end to an isolation which was a major psychological handicap to even the hardiest immigrant. Few had really been prepared for the loneliness of carving a new life out of the untamed and largely unpopulated bush. The railways spelled ready access to other settlements and cities which would make settlers not only richer, but less lonely as well. And so, when the railway came, there was always a party. William Armstrong was often commissioned to record these events and paint the celebrations at the opening of new rail lines.

Above, the opening of the Toronto and Nipissing Railway at Uxbridge, September 14, 1871.

Right, Prince Arthur's visit to Weston for the Toronto, Grey and Bruce Railway sod-turning, October 6, 1869.

20

Laying the cornerstone of the Union Station, Toronto, June, 1872.

The first Union Station was replaced in 1873 by a magnificent new building which became one of the best known structures in Toronto, where many new and impressive buildings were being constructed. The Grand Trunk Railway used the new station, but the other lines also employed it as their terminus.

The coming of the railways to Canada West meant the coming of Standard Time. This proposal which was made by Sandford Fleming, a life-long friend of William Armstrong, did much to regularize com-

merce and travel from east to west in Canada. So also did the adoption of a uniform width for Canadian railway tracks. Before this was done, as many as three rails ran into the station, and railway companies had their choice of which track they would use.

Clearing a snow drift on the Grand Trunk line, near Stratford, December, 1871.

Train travel was often hazardous. In summer there were errant deer; in spring and fall the hazards included wind-felled trees; and in winter drifting snow was a constant problem. But there were few disasters as tragic as that in which a Great Western train crashed through a bridge near Hamilton in March, 1857, plunged into a canal and seventy lives were lost.

Life in Victorian Toronto

William Armstrong's involvement in the life of Toronto was immediate and extensive. The city was growing at a tremendous rate. In 1834 it was incorporated as a city of 9,000 people; when Armstrong arrived in 1851 the population was 30,000, and immigrants of diverse backgrounds and religions were busily sorting themselves into a stratified social structure. Armstrong must have almost instantly committed himself to his new homeland because he played a prominent part in this burgeoning social and artistic life.

By 1871, Toronto's population had reached 56,000, and with the expansion of the city, the older areas began to be neglected. Toronto was reflecting the spirit of the age as it began its westward spread along the shores of Lake Ontario. The 1850's had seen the building of University College, Osgoode Hall, old Trinity Church, St. James and St. Michael's cathedrals and many other buildings which survive today as evidence of how the immigrants imported the heavy, yet often graceful, architecture of Victorian England. When Sandford Fleming and Collingwood Schreiber built a provincial exhibition building, it was quite nat-

ural that they should model it on the Crystal Palace built in London for the Great Exposition of 1851.

Inevitably, the lake itself played a dominant role in the life of Toronto; the city began with the building of Fort Rouillé (commonly known as Fort Toronto) in 1749 as a trading post readily accessible by water. With a natural harbour provided by the sandbar in the Toronto Bay which curled, crescent like, from the mainland, Toronto's *raison d'être* had long been that it was a trading centre for the hinterland settlements.

It was probably also inevitable that a man raised as a boy near Dublin Harbour should be irresistibly attracted to a lake which is, after all, more accurately described as an inland sea. Armstrong was among the first members of the Yacht Club of Toronto, which, in 1854, became the Royal Canadian Yacht Club — by permission of Queen Victoria herself. In later years he was an officer and then a life member of the club.

Much of his painting reflects his involvement with the harbour and the island; with the yacht club which he helped establish; with the industrial and building activities which were the visible signs of the economic changes in Canada West.

Left, the wreck of the schooner Sophia, *1866 (detail).*

24

By 1850 shipping had become so important to Toronto that a Harbour Commission was set up to regulate the use of the Queen's Wharf, and the harbour was busy with scheduled mail and passenger steamers as well as sailing schooners used as cargo boats for grain and timber. As this traffic declined in the face of competition from the railways, so the harbour became more of a recreational centre and home of pleasure craft. The view of the city from Toronto Island appealed to William Armstrong, and he painted it often. The Toronto Island was actually a peninsula linked at its eastern end to the mainland until, in 1858, a raging storm washed away buildings and embankments built on low-lying land, and slashed a 500-foot gap in the sandbar. The peninsula became Toronto's islands.

The prize winning lithograph, a panorama of Toronto as seen from the peninsula, 1856.

William Armstrong enjoyed the days he spent sailing
Toronto harbour and Lake Ontario in his boat the 3A, seen
above (detail of painting) beached on Toronto Island.

   As an engineer, he was fascinated by the task of laying
water mains from the Toronto Island pumping station after a
bad break in the conduit pipe under the bay caused it to float
to the surface. In 1898 a new seventy-two-inch steel intake
pipe (left) was completed across the harbour to the city.

29

The Chief Justice Robinson *landing passengers on the ice in Toronto Bay, 1852-53.*

Boatworks at the foot of Bathurst Street, 1865.

32

The Provincial, *headquarters of the Yacht Club, in the ice in Toronto Bay, about 1869.*

William Armstrong probably painted the picture at left with more–or at least different–feeling than he brought to his other work. It is of the steamer *Provincial*, which gave him many sleepless nights. She was a wreck bought in 1860 by the Royal Canadian Yacht Club, moored on the bay shore and then used as a clubhouse. But the once-wrecked *Provincial* was jinxed. As Armstrong later recalled: "Often I was called up in the middle of the night with the information that she had broken loose, and then I had to go down and put in the rest of the night getting her fast again." When Armstrong joined the Yacht Club in 1852, it had been in existence only two years. When, in 1854, members decided to ask Queen Victoria for permission to use the prefix "Royal," many Torontonians considered them presumptuous. In August of that year, however, an aide to the Governor General told club members that "Her Majesty was graciously pleased to comply with their prayer." But the newly dignified club retained the errant *Provincial* as a headquarters until 1869.

Royal tours of Victorian Canada were major milestones in the nation's history, and when the Prince of Wales, later King Edward VII, visited Toronto by water in September, 1860, Royal Canadian Yacht Club members and other yachtsmen-citizens jammed the harbour in their craft and, in a dramatically colourful display of flags and finery, "dressed ship" to greet the Prince as he arrived aboard the steamer Kingston. Later the Prince presented the Royal Canadian Yacht Club with a trophy to commemorate his visit.

The Prince of Wales visits Toronto, Sept. 7, 1860.

Choppy water on Lake Ontario, 1880 (detail).

Left, the **Vreda***, winning the Queen's Cup, 1894.*

OVERLEAF. *The* **Oriole II***, owned by Commodore G. Gooderham.*

Above, racing on Lake Ontario, 1884.

Left, the yacht Cyprus, *1889.*

The Coral, *1873.*

Left, the yacht Verve I.

In the farm lands and bush country beyond the city limits, men and women struggled to open new settlements and cope with the rugged climate. History has come to see this as an epic phase in the story of Canada. But in the city, life was, on its facade, at least, a facsimile of Victorian England.

William Armstrong recorded the events of the day, and one of these was the unveiling of the monument to the men who fell in the Battle of Ridgeway in 1866. Armstrong became involved in the 10th Regiment of Royal Grenadiers of Toronto, a company recruited from among the artisans and professional groups of the city. While he probably did not participate in the expedition from Toronto to Fort Erie and the disastrous engagement at Ridgeway, he was a close associate of many in the company.

In one of his most dramatic paintings, Armstrong recorded the Toronto Rolling Mills, which at the time was the largest manufacturing industry in the city.

Unveiling the Ridgeway Monument, Queen's Park, Toronto, July 1, 1870.

OVERLEAF. *Toronto Rolling Mills, 1864.*

Armstrong
1861

FROM THE CANADIAN ILLUSTRATED NEWS

Victorian Toronto's unswerving loyalty to British traditions and to the Crown was reflected in the patriotic flags and bunting used to decorate the Toronto Racket Court for a grand ball in 1871.

Niagara Falls from the south side of the American Falls.

Niagara

Strong men have been known to fall silent with awe at their first sight of Niagara Falls. Others wax eloquent, as did American naturalist and artist John J. Audubon, who wrote: "All the pictures you may see, all the descriptions you may read of these mighty Falls can only produce in your mind the faint glimmer of the glowworm compared with the overpowering glory of the meridian sun." The work of William Armstrong, whose comments go unrecorded, suggests that he found the Falls entrancing, but that as an engineer his imagination was also captured by the handiwork of man which surrounds them. Presumably he found the construction of the first suspension bridge over the Niagara River gorge particularly interesting, since it had been built with the aid of a small boy only three years prior to Armstrong's arrival in Canada. The builder, Charles Ellett, offered a prize to anyone who could fly a kite from one side of the gorge to the other. The next windy day a horde of small boys stood flying kites on the American side. When one landed on the Canadian shore, the string was used to haul a rope over, and the rope to haul a wire cable which was, in fact, the bridge, since the crossing was accomplished in a basket built for two suspended from the cable.

On both American and Canadian sides of the Falls, Armstrong recorded the commercial uses to which the resources of the area had been put. He appears to have been fascinated, too, by other structures of man, such as the ruins of Fort Mississauga erected in Niagara-on-the-Lake by the British after their defeat of the Americans in 1813. And Armstrong the engineer and bridge-builder must have had mixed feelings when he painted a picture of the tower built on rocks near Goat Island so tourists could look down over the Horseshoe Fall: the tower was reached by a perilously rickety bridge from the mainland.

Geologists say it must have taken the Niagara River more than 70,000 years to carve out the seven-mile-long gorge which runs from the Falls' present location to Lake Ontario, so there can have been little change in the Falls we see now and those William Armstrong first saw more than a century ago. However, there was one tourist attraction at the Falls then that is missing today: in the mid-1800's you could actually walk *behind* the cataract on the Canadian side. Mr. Barnett, who ran the Niagara Falls Museum, would provide oilskins and a guide to lead you behind the blanket of water and its stinging spray. And if tourists lacked the courage to make that trip, Mr. Barnett would still get his tourist dollar from the museum, which had a collection of ancient coins and displays of stuffed buffaloes, rattlesnakes, a barbary lion, monkeys, and other fauna, including well-mounted specimens of a bird called the glutton and the duck-billed platypus.

Fort Niagara, American side of Lake Ontario, 1891.

*During the American Revolution the British were forced
to abandon Fort Niagara on the south side of Lake Ontario.
To replace it, they built Fort George in the town today called
Niagara-on-the-Lake, once the capital of Upper Canada.*

*In 1813 American invaders destroyed Fort George and
the town, and after driving them back across the river, the
British built Fort Mississauga. Because of his interest in
recording these military monuments, William Armstrong
painted Fort Niagara on the American side of the lake, and
the ruins of Fort Mississauga on the Canadian side.*

Fort Mississauga, 1891.

Until bridges were built people crossed the river below Niagara Falls by ferry in summer and by foot across the ice in winter, when paths were carefully marked and refreshment booths were set up in mid-passage. In winter, the Falls were a wonderland of ice and frost. One writer of the 1880's said of them: "Glittering wreaths of icicles gleam on the brow of every projecting rock and jutting crag. Every fallen fragment of rock under its icy covering becomes a marble column, and masses of frozen spray stand out in graceful form, easily shaped by the imagination into the half-finished work of a sculptor."

Frozen railway water-tower (above) on the Canadian bank of the Niagara River.

The American Falls (opposite), seen from the Canadian side.

By far the most spectacular method of crossing the Falls and the Niagara River was that chosen by Jean Francois Gravelet, better known as Blondin. Born in France in 1824, he earned a place in the lexicon of dare-devilry by crossing the Falls and the river on a tightrope in 1859. For his next trick, and the ones after that, he stood balanced on the wire halfway across; hung from it first by his hands and then by his feet; lowered himself to the boiling surface of the water; trundled a wheelbarrow across on the wire, and even hobbled across it in a sack. And when, in 1860, the Prince of Wales visited Niagara, Blondin even gave a Royal Command Performance on his wire.

But bridging the Falls and the Niagara River gorge in a more practical manner was one of the major achievements of the Victorian era. The first suspension bridge across the gorge near the Falls was built in 1867-68 near the Clifton Hotel. It was 1,260 feet long and swayed alarmingly above the swirling river 192 feet below. It was rebuilt and widened in 1888, but the next January it blew down.

Then a safer bridge with steel cables, towers and a stiffening truss was built, but it, too, was quickly superseded: a steel arch bridge was built in 1899. That endured until 1938, when it was destroyed by ice, but it was not replaced until the Rainbow Bridge was opened in 1941.

A mile-and-a-half downriver from the Falls a railroad suspension bridge was built in 1856, but twenty years earlier, engineers had drawn up plans for a suspension bridge at Queenston much farther down the gorge in the direction of Lake Ontario. Work didn't actually begin on that project until 1850. The bridge opened the following year–and it was destroyed by a storm thirteen years later. The bridge supports had been removed for fear of an ice jam, and the weakened structure couldn't withstand the howling winds.

The Niagara River where it empties into Lake Ontario, painted by William Armstrong in 1898. This view, from Queenston Heights, shows the railway lines — at right and at left — on the Canadian and American sides.

OVERLEAF. *Blondin crosses the Niagara River near the Falls, 1859.*

Indians fishing, North Shore, Lake Huron.

Great Lakes Travels

Lake Huron, Georgian Bay

o modern Canada, the value of William Armstrong's aintings and drawings is not only his considerable rtistic talent, but the attention to accuracy which, s an engineer, was part of his nature. This placed im outside the mainstream of the art of his time, for nost of the artists who painted pioneer and Victo-an Canada did so in the European Romantic style.

As a topographical artist, Armstrong departed from ne popular decorative style of many European illus-ators who prepared works that were reproduced in ngravings or lithographs in England. William Henry artlett, the British illustrator who toured Canada and merica between 1835 and the time Armstrong rrived in Toronto in 1851, was a man whose widely ublished work is an example of the rose-tinted ver-on of Canada these artists left behind them. Edwin Vhitefield, from the United States, was more con-erned with accurate delineation, and was a com-anion of Armstrong in this regard. W. S. Hunter was Canadian whose topographical views of Ottawa, the astern Townships and Niagara Falls were much in emand from 1855 to 1870.

William Armstrong's work is almost photographic a its honesty. The bleak and forbidding beauty of the nd around the Great Lakes, Lake Nipigon and other arts of that area then known as Canada West was yet rgely unknown to Victorian Canada, which, in the nid-1800's, was focused around Quebec, the Mari-me provinces and Lake Ontario. Armstrong con-eived it his duty to accurately represent the land he as fortunate to see as a railway engineer, private aveller and member of the Red River Expedition. He ainted it as it was–indeed, as it still often is. onsequently, his rivers are not gently pastoral but onest torrents; his lakes don't glassily reflect mirror nages, but are bodies of often treacherous water.

Armstrong visited Lake Nipigon and the surround-ing countryside in 1867 and 1869. So did some Ameri-cans, whose accounts of their travels led the *New York Citizen and Round Table* to say that Nipigon country was "as much a terra incognita as Central Africa." Armstrong helped change that state of affairs, but even today no one who sees his paintings and then visits the actual sites could accuse him of glamouriz-ing them.

The same is true of his many paintings depicting the customs of nomadic Indian tribes. He recorded many details of their way of life, not with the romantic curiosity of Anna Jamieson or the eye for costume and ornament of Paul Kane, but with a determination to record their hunting and living habits.

Though he painted scenes from Canada West throughout his life, most of Armstrong's travels to the head of the Great Lakes took place in his first twenty years in Canada, and in the main, he travelled in the relative comfort of the ships which called at the com-munities grown up around trading posts established long before by the Hudson's Bay and North West Companies. Even so, it was no small adventure, for travel by lake steamer was often dangerous: the *Niagara* was lost on September 24, 1856, near Port Washington with the loss of many lives. It was not uncommon for the engineers to prepare their wills before setting out from Toronto on Lake Huron. Armstrong was travelling the area at the time–and the *Niagara* tragedy wasn't exactly an exceptional event. And once Armstrong had disembarked at Sault Ste. Marie or Prince Arthur's Landing, or any of the other ports of call for the streamers, the onward jour-ney was inevitably long and uncomfortable; the accomodation available primitive; the land he saw a challenge to strong men.

Top. Indians spearing sturgeon, Lake Huron.

Bottom. Little Current, Manitoulin Island.

n Indian camp on Manitoulin Island, Georgian Bay.

The paintings and drawings on the following pages are the product of Armstrong's Odyssey around the upper Great Lakes, which really began when, in 1856, the first railway from Toronto reached Georgian Bay and the rail-head terminus of Hen and Chicken's Harbour became Collingwood, jumping-off point for the hinterland. The paintings were not produced in tidy sequence, but, as presented here, they represent a step-by-step record of Armstrong's travels, beginning with Lake Huron and Georgian Bay and moving onward, northward and westward to the remote reaches of Lake Superior.

On the north channel of Georgian Bay, just east of Manitoulin Island, was the settlement of Shebanwanning, now Killarney, Ontario. The steamer in the distance is going through the North Channel, heading for Manitoulin Island. The land on the left is George Island. Shebanwanning was a regular port of call for the coastal boats. It provided a dispatch point for the Indian fishermen, who could put their catch on board and secure supplies there.

In 1835 there were only seventy or eighty Indians on Manitoulin Island; government officers recorded five or six families of the Ottawa, or Odaway, tribe from Lake Michigan, plus a few wandering Chippewas. In 1836, the government began to build a settlement on the island, and two years later, the first white settlers, mostly labourers and tradesmen, began to winter there. By 1860, the population of the island was about six hundred.

Each year there were great gatherings of the tribes at a pre-determined point on the island so that the representative of the government could distribute the gifts that had to be provided by the terms of the treaties with the Indians.

The settlement of Shebanwanning, now Killarney, Ontario.

When Armstrong painted the last treaty gathering held on Manitoulin in 1856 (overleaf), the white man had built houses, schools and churches and encouraged the tribes to settle. Chief Assigenack is shown naming the Indians to Captain Ironside, the Indian Superintendent. The view includes the schoolmaster and his wife, the postmaster and a Jesuit missionary.

Last century saw the slow and painful and often bloody curtailing of the Indian's freedom to wander his native North America. By treaty, force and–too rarely–friendly persuasion, the tribes were confined to reserves in both America and Canada, so that the vast land over which they roamed could be laid open for the westward thrust of European settlers and European civilization. The Manitoulin Island which William Armstrong painted time and time again was one of the better examples of government policy which, today, many people say caged and helped destroy the Indian spirit. The British government cleared land, built shack-like houses, churches, schools, and tried to help Indians start industries that would encourage them to support themselves in the white man's economy. Lieutenant-Governor Sir Francis Bond Head's policy was to collect all Indians north of Lake Huron and in Upper Canada and give them "Indians-only" land on Manitoulin, which is about a hundred miles long and four to twenty-five miles wide.

An Indian camp, Georgian Bay.

Indians fishing with nets in the St. Mary's River, Sault Ste. Marie.

Perhaps because they saw what they wanted to, government officers reported that tribes settled on Manitoulin Island lost much of their desire to leave the island and go hunting and fishing. But some did leave, and, in fact, not all Indians would settle on the island. And where these people set up camp, it was possible to see the traditional tee-pees and a life-style which had remained unchanged for centuries. William Armstrong never tired of painting scenes such as this one. His unemotional honesty in doing so makes his pictures an invaluable social record, and part of the heritage of Canada and its Indians.

Readying the canoe at an Indian camp, Georgian Bay.

The northern Great Lakes are now acknowledged to be the richest source of mineral wealth in the northern part of the continent. But there were rich copper mines on Lake Huron long before the first great rush of prospectors into the area in the 1860's. The Bruce Mines west of Manitoulin Island on the north shore of Lake Huron were active in the late 1840's and were not abandoned until the 1870's. A dozen shafts went down about 300 feet to the ore body, and as many as 300 men worked in the crude underground galleries. The ore they dug was crushed at the mine, then shipped to Swansea in Wales for smelting. In later years, some of the ore was sent to new smelters in Buffalo, New York.

Bruce Mines Landing, on the north shore of Lake Huron.

Where the railways that William Armstrong helped build left off, the Great Lakes steamships took over. Goods and passengers would be transported to lakeside towns like Collingwood on Georgian Bay, and would then be transferred to boats like the *City of Owen Sound* and the *Campana,* to make the often perilous voyages farther in to the interior. Most of Armstrong's travelling to the area of northern Lake Superior was done aboard these ships, which were every bit as important as the railways in the opening up of Canada West.

The steamers City of Owen Sound *(above) and* Campana *(opposite) plied the Great Lakes.*

The **Ploughboy**, *which nearly went aground on July 1, 1859, with Sir John A. Macdonald aboard.*

Canadian history might read differently today if the United States had not gone ahead–despite the fact that many considered it a pointless project–and built a ship canal linking Lakes Huron and Superior. In 1851-52, the American Congress approved plans for the canal which, as Henry Clay said in Washington at the time, "is a work beyond the remotest settlement of the United States, if not the moon."

The mile-long canal took two gruelling years to build and at one time between 1,200 and 1,500 men worked on the project. The Red River Rebellion was settled by the arrival of Colonel Wolseley's troops, which set off from Toronto in May and arrived at Fort Garry in August. The ships of the expedition moved from one lake to the other through the two 350-foot-long locks of the American canal.

Colonel Wolseley's men landing at Sault Ste. Marie on their way to Fort Garry.

Armstrong's most memorable trip north was as a member of Colonel Wolseley's Red River Expedition, sent to subdue the Riel Rebellion at Fort Garry. The expedition's ships went through the American canal at Sault Ste. Marie empty, while the troops camped on Canadian territory (overleaf).

1870-1913

The American side of Sault Ste. Marie as it appeared in 1871.

The Hudson's Bay Company post at Sault Ste. Marie.

Indian camp by the American canal between Lakes Huron and Superior.

Nipigon

FROM THE CANADIAN ILLUSTRATED NEWS

La Roche que Frappe, a towering headland which leans out over the lake ten to fourteen feet from the vertical, could be seen from a Hudson's Bay Company post which Armstrong visited when he travelled on Lake Nipigon.

When Armstrong first visited the Nipigon region, maps of Canada either didn't show Lake Nipigon, or showed it as little more than a pond. The first accounts spelled it in various manners, mainly Neepigon. From Armstrong's sketches and the reports of geologist Bell, newspapers and periodicals of the time produced accounts which made Nipigon country sound like the Promised Land. The lake and river teemed with fish; the mineral deposits were undoubtedly rich; the land was fertile—though, as one con

FROM THE CANADIAN ILLUSTRATED NEWS

A view south from High Rock Portage.

temporary reporter pointed out, winter lasted nearly six months "and [that] prepares us to hear that Indian Corn will not ripen in that neighbourhood; nor even wheat, except in favourable seasons." Lake Nipigon was reported to be the sixth and last in the Great Lakes chain, possibly bigger than Lake Ontario, or even Lake Erie.

When William Armstrong went to Nipigon as a member of government survey parties in 1867 and 1869, only the Hudson's Bay Company agents, who ran a trading post there, and local Indians really knew the region. A strait and a bay on the north shore of Lake Huron, and a river leading to the island-dotted Lake Nipigon itself all bear the name Nipigon, and the drawings done by Armstrong were to make the country better known. They were used as the basis for illustrations published in *The Canadian Illustrated News* in 1870.

View of the Nipigon River.

FROM THE CANADIAN ILLUSTRATED NEWS

Hudson's Bay Company post on the northwest shore of Lake Nipigon.

Lake Nipigon was a rich and profitable trading area for the Hudson's Bay Company. While not as big as Armstrong and early surveyors at first believed, it is, as a missionary said at the time, so wide that "the land of one coast is entirely invisible from that of the other." By Armstrong's time, Indians and white men were at peace, but in earlier years the H.B.C. had fortified posts around the lakeshore. As an observer described these posts: "They were once block-houses or fortifications against the hostile natives, and from one to the other of these the various goods and peltries are transmitted by canoes and canoemen, who ply forward and back almost like ferryboats. These stations were once about a day's journey apart, but of late years many of them have been discontinued where all danger from enemies has disappeared."

ROM THE CANADIAN ILLUSTRATED NEWS

A view from High Rock Portage, looking north from the head of the Pechaunigum Rapids.

Miss De La Ronde, daughter of the post superintendent, with Ojibway canoes at the Hudson's Bay Company post on Lake Nipigon.

Indians portaging a canoe over a difficult area on a trip along the Nipigon River.

An Indian encampment at the mouth of the Black Sturgeon River, looking east.

he Black Sturgeon River; a view looking south.

Two men could carry the standard birch-bark canoe, as in this case at the portage of the Pechaunigum Rapids on the Nipigon River.

Northwest Lake Superior

On May 25, 1870, the steamer *Chicora* sailed past Thunder Cape, a sentinel of rock which rears with brutal suddenness out of the northwest end of Lake Superior and looks, from the shore, like nothing so much as a sleeping giant. The vanguard of the Red River Expedition had arrived at Thunder Bay.

It had taken five days to travel from Toronto–and that was possible only because the railway now ran north from the city to Collingwood on Georgian Bay; because the railway had encouraged the development of Great Lakes navigation; and because the *Chicora* had been able to use the American canal linking Lakes Huron and Superior. During the next several days the rest of the expedition's ships, including the *Algoma* and the *Brooklyn,* were to arrive. Then the brutal, overland stage of the journey to Fort Garry to subdue Louis Riel and his followers began.

Colonel Garnet Wolseley landed his men at what was then called Dawson's Landing, a tiny mining community. He lost no time in renaming it Prince Arthur's Landing in honour of Prince Arthur, Duke of Connaught, whose regiment was part of the expedition. Wolseley had to move his guns, supplies, troops and their voyageur, Indian and civilian followers–William Armstrong included–through almost fifty miles of bush to Lake Shebandowan, the next navigable stretch of water to carry the expedition farther westward to Fort Garry, Riel's headquarters.

How this was done is an epic of Canadian history. The troops built roads; explored uncharted rivers; braved hitherto un-navigated rapids; set about rebuilding bridges destroyed in a forest fire which had raged through the area only a week earlier. They finally got through to Shebandowan, and in August reached Fort Garry. The rebellion was quashed, and Riel had fled.

The steamer Algoma, *sister ship of the* Chicora, *transporting troops past Thunder Cape on the Red River Expedition, May, 1870.*

Thunder Cape, guardian of Thunder Bay, 1867.

The Dawson Road station at the south end of Lake Shebandowan.

Mr. Molyneux St. John, Toronto newspaper correspondent for the Globe, *and his wife run the Island Rapids on the Sturgeon River. The couple accompanied the Red River Expedition.*

*Colonel Wolseley waiting for the completion of the
Dawson Road at his camp at Prince Arthur's Landing.
With most of his Red River Expedition camped and waiting,
Colonel Wolseley found that the Dawson Road, which
headed in the direction of Lake Shebandowan, was in good
order for twenty-six miles—but then petered out. The course
of the road ran through rough country, but his troops began
the task of finishing it. This proceeded slowly, however, and
so Wolseley abandoned the road-making and had his men
undertake the rest of the way to Fort Garry by portage route.*

Cashabowie Station, transport point at the head of Lake Shebandowan, start of the journey for the troops across the lake.

The Great Dog portage, Dog Lake was an alternate route for transporting supplies from Fort William to Fort Garry.

A temporary fort (left) was constructed at Prince Arthur's Landing to store the ammunition and provisions of the expedition.

OVERLEAF. *One of the more difficult portages at Deux Rivières. Wooden trestles were built and the 150 heavy boats of the expedition were pushed along them by hand.*

Indian canoes with travellers returning from the west were steered with poles and paddles down the Kaministiquia River. The travellers, mainly fur traders and prospectors, had exciting tales to tell to the people of the more settled areas of Canada West, and their adventures and experiences became well known. But William Armstrong, through his painting, provided a visual record of the area and the way of life of the nomadic Indian tribes that lived there.

Travelling on the Kaministiquia River.

Kakabeka Falls, on the Kaministiquia River, provides a formidable barrier to transportation. The river in its course to Fort William meets a barrier of rock over which it tumbles more than 100 feet to the gorge below. The spray at the foot of the Falls does not rise in a large cloud, as at Niagara. It shoots into the air at a sharp angle with great velocity and repeated noise, giving the impression of a series of explosions. From Kakabeka Falls, the Kaministiquia River rushes in torrents to Lake Superior, dropping a height of over a hundred feet in a relatively short distance.

Mouth of the Current River.

Fishing on the Mackenzie River, Thunder Bay.

Prince Arthur's Landing in 1872.

July. 30 . 72

FROM THE CANADIAN ILLUSTRATED NEWS

Prince Arthur's Landing (renamed Port Arthur about 1883) on the shores of Lake Superior, 1872.

View of Fort William, at the mouth of the Kaministiquia River. The town was selected as the starting point for construction of the Pacific Railway to the west.

Sir George Simpson's canoe at the Hudson's Bay post, Fort William. Before the days of the lake steamships, Simpson made his regular trips from Montreal to the post in this canoe.

Silver Island in Lake Superior, lying in the distance, as seen from the mainland.

The great push westward had begun by the time William Armstrong reached Canada, but in the next twenty years it was to be given greater impetus by the first evidence that great mineral storehouses in the upper Great Lakes were just waiting to be mined to feed the machines of industrial Europe and North America. In 1863, Armstrong acquired 120 acres of land with mineral rights on the Kaministiquia River.

As well as any, Silver Island symbolized the discoveries which fired the imagination of Victorian Canada. The island was just a hundred feet long and forty feet wide, and most of that was submerged at high water, when all that could be seen was a large rock about eight feet high. But in 1868, Thomas MacFarlane discovered a rich vein of silver in that rock–and Silver Island became famous.

Early attempts to mine the silver failed because the lake flooded the mine shafts. Then Captain William Frue, an American citizen of Portage Lake, bought it and surrounded the island with a breakwater and pumped out the water. Six men started digging–and in four days took out $35,000 worth of silver. It was a widely publicized bonanza, and in December, 1870, the *Duluth Minnesotan* reported excitedly: "Already 123 barrels of native silver, estimated to be worth $75,000 to $100,000 have been shipped. Eye-witnesses of intelligence, judgment and experience report that Capt. Frue will probably take out of Silver Island, up to the opening of navigation next spring, from $1,000,000 to $3,000,000 in money value."

It was one of the richest silver mines in the world and it was abandoned when, in 1880, the 1,300-foot-deep shaft began flooding at the rate of 105 gallons of lakewater a minute. It was said that the last miner to leave could see $300,000 worth of silver in the roof of the shaft and couldn't reach it.

In Victorian Canada most men went to the Great Lakes with eyes only for its wealth. Fortunately for posterity William Armstrong, the engineer who did much to make this wealth accessible, also looked with the eye of an artist.

Amethyst Falls, Mackenzie River, Thunder Bay.

Over one hundred years have elapsed since William Armstrong first painted scenes of the Great Lakes and of the lands and waterways around them. Although French fur traders and missionaries preceded William Armstrong and the railroad exploring parties of the nineteenth century by over two hundred years, they did not provide anything like the extensive visual record of the later groups. By his work, William Armstrong recorded in a unique fashion much of what we know today concerning the early life in the Great Lakes region, particularly during the period 1856 to 1880.

In 1912, just two years before he died, William Armstrong was asked by the National Gallery of Canada to provide some account of his work as an artist. He wrote, "I was laughed at when I said that Sault Ste. Marie, Fort William and Port Arthur would be great cities. What changes I have seen in 61 years."

It was this realization—that the scenes he saw around him would be transformed beyond recogni-

On the Mackenzie River, Thunder Bay.

tion-that led William Armstrong to document the life of his time. Because he did so, the transformations which took place as the land was opened up for settlement are now more clearly appreciated.

Canada has been called a land where as much of its past can be learned from a canoe as from a history book. William Armstrong understood very well that portaging a canoe overland between two stretches of water was a characteristic activity of the new land. After one hundred years, the canoe is still a basic means of penetrating much of Canada.

As Canadians by the tens of thousands travel over the rivers and waterways around the Great Lakes, the Victorian views of William Armstrong do not seem out of place. While the methods of travelling may have altered, the attraction of the landscape remains as strong as ever. The paintings and sketches of William Armstrong, artist and civil engineer, always will command attention and understanding from those who travel in the path of the voyageurs.

Index to Illustrations

Picture Credits

After the first recording, principal sources are credited under the following abbreviations:

GA   Glenbow Alberta Institute, Calgary
JRR   John Ross Robertson Collection, Metropolitan Toronto Central Library
MTLB   Metropolitan Toronto Library Board
PAC   Public Archives of Canada, Ottawa
RCYC   Royal Canadian Yacht Club, Toronto
SSC   Sigmund Samuel Collection, Royal Ontario Museum, Toronto
THB   Toronto Historical Board

Half title Mrs. P. C. Band, Toronto; title Mrs. P. C. Band; acknowledgements Public Archives of Canada, Ottawa; 10 private collection; 11 John Ross Robertson Collection, Metropolitan Toronto Central Library; 12 Toronto and Early Canada Collection, Metropolitan Toronto Central Library; H. C. Campbell, Toronto; 13 JRR; 14 Sigmund Samuel Collection, Royal Ontario Museum, Toronto; 16/17 private collection; 18 SSC; 18/19 PAC; 20 Metropolitan Toronto Library Board; 21 MTLB; 22 JRR; 24/25 SSC; 26 private collection; 26/27 private collection; 28/29 JRR; 30/31 Mrs. P. C. Band; 32/33 JRR; 34/35 The National Gallery of Canada, Ottawa; 36/37 Royal Canadian Yacht Club, Toronto; 37 JRR; 38/39 RCYC; 40/41 Toronto Historical Board; 41 RCYC; 42 Mrs. P. C. Band; 43 RCYC; 44/45 MTLB; 46/47 JRR; 48/49 MTLB; 50 Mrs. P. C. Band; 52 PAC; 53 PAC; 54/55 Mrs. P. C. Band; 55 SSC; 56/57 Mrs. P. C. Band; 58/59 SSC; 60 Glenbow Alberta Institute, Calgary; 62 PAC; 63 Mrs. P. C. Band; 64/65 JRR; 66/67 Laing Gallery, Toronto; 68/69 Mrs. P. C. Band; 70/71 PAC; 72/73 GA; 74/75 PAC; 76/77 MTLB; 78 THB; 78/79 THB; 80 JRR; 81 JRR; 82/83 JRR; 84 JRR; 85 JRR; 86/87 PAC; 88 MTLB; 89 MTLB; 90/91 PAC; 92 MTLB; 93 MTLB; 94 Mrs. P. C. Band; 95 Dr. F. A. L. Mathewson, Winnipeg; 96 MTLB; 97 MTLB; 98/99 PAC; 100/101 MTLB; 102/103 PAC; 104 MTLB; 105 SSC; 106 PAC; 107 PAC; 108/109 MTLB; 109 GA; 110/111 Winnipeg Art Gallery; 112/113 Sotheby & Co. (Canada) Ltd., Toronto; 114/115 Mrs. P. C. Band; 116 Dr. F. A. L. Mathewson; 117 GA; 118/119 Mrs. P. C. Band; 120 MTLB; 121 JRR; 122/123 Mrs. P. C. Band; 124/125 PAC; 126 PAC; 127 PAC.